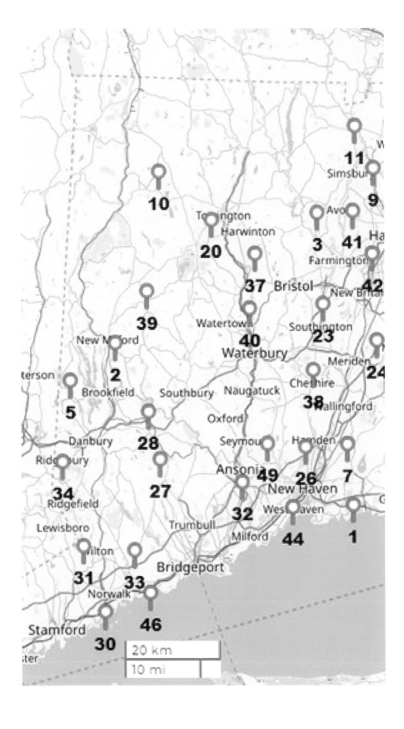

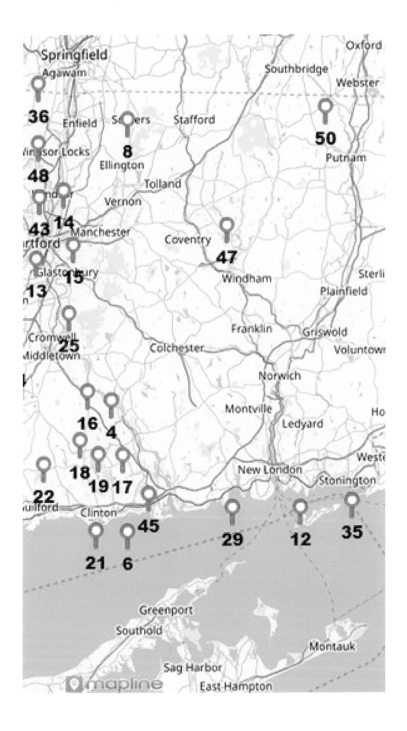

Chasing Labyrinths

# Chasing Labyrinths

## A Field Guide to Labyrinths of
## Connecticut and Rhode Island

Bill Ludwig

Hotchkiss Publishing

2020

CIP

Copyright © 2020 Wm. J. Ludwig

ISBN: 978-0-9909020-7-2


Edited by: Stephen Smolka
Design: Karin Badger
Layout/Production: Liz Delton
Maps: Mapline.com


First edition: May 2020
*Printed in the United States of America*


*Published by:*

HOTCHKISS PUBLISHING
17 Frank Street
Branford, CT 06405
info@HotchkissPublishing.com
www.HotchkissPublishing.com

Cover Photo: Holy Family Retreat Labyrinth West Hartford, CT

# *Dedication*

*For Eric who inspires me daily
and the Charlottes in our lives.*

# Contents

# Acknowledgments

I would like to thank Walter Kawecki and Steve Smolka for starting me on this journey, the World Wide Labyrinth Locator and The Labyrinth Society for providing direction along the way. Steve also was good enough to take the time from his own book to help edit my writing. Rick Ludwig offered much need perspective and encouragement. Charlotte van Essen who has walked many labyrinths with me and has provided love and support from the start. Of course, I want to thank all of the people who share their labyrinths and stories in this volume for their time, kindness, and support.

# Preface

## My Labyrinth Story

Early in 2016 I was working on volume two of *Dear Friend, spiritual meditations and journal* written by Sandy Beach. All of my designer's cover mockups were nice but not quite what I wanted. When I mentioned my frustration to a friend, he suggested a website for me to search which offered high-quality photos. My first search under "spiritual path" returned a stunning photo of a beach labyrinth being walked by a lone person. I sent it to my designer and soon had the perfect cover. This led me to look into the significance of labyrinths and how they differed from mazes. Gradually I was drawn to learn more. When I discovered the World Labyrinth Locator website, I was thrilled to find one in the town where I was born. So, it was on January 1st, 2017, that I walked my first labyrinth at the First Church of Christ in Woodbridge, CT. I've continued to use the Locator website when I travel and have since added dozens of labyrinths to my "Life List".

A few months following my introduction to labyrinths I found myself being called to another very different meditative walk. The Camino de Santiago beckoned when I began following a friend's blog as he completed his pilgrimage across Spain in the Spring of 2016. When he returned home, I peppered him for information and soon was making plans for my own pilgrimage. Researching labyrinths on the Camino, I found only a few references to mostly temporary or spontaneous installations.

October 15, 2017, I departed Lourdes, France and walked 1000 kilometers over 47 days to Santiago de Compostela, Spain. I was nearly halfway before encountering my first labyrinth. I was walking that day with two Dutch women, Charlotte & Janny, who I had just met that morning as we were leaving the albergue in Villafranchi Montes de Oca when mid-morning, we came upon two identical spiral labyrinths side by side made of stones. When I said that I wanted to pause to walk one of them, Charlotte said that she would walk the other. When we finished, she had a huge smile on her face and I had tears running down my cheeks! I told her that she had apparently walked the happy one and I had chosen the sad one.

Later, during lunch, Janny announced that she had needed to stop for the day. However, Charlotte had to continue so she could reach Burgos in two days to make her travel connections home to The Netherlands. We went off from there together, enjoying each other's company, until we arrived at Cruz de Matagrande, the highest point in this section of the Camino, where we discovered a giant labyrinth. This was another spiral pattern to which passing pilgrims have been obviously adding stones for some time. We decided to take a 20-minute break, from our westward walk, to walk to the center of the labyrinth. Charlotte began and I followed about 10 feet behind her. Both of us remaining silent the entire way. When she reached the center she turned, opened her arms, and into them I walked. It was then that our souls collided and we discovered ourselves connected. This was remarkable because to that point neither of us realized we were even interested in the other.

We had only been together a total of 48 hours when she returned home, leaving me alone in Burgos with 500 kilometers still to walk and ponder what had just happened. As of this writing I have become a frequent flyer to Holland and she has made numerous visits to the USA, the future looks bright. Last October, we spent a lovely weekend in Paris during which we visited the Cathedral in Chartres. There we walked the historic labyrinth on the Cathedral floor and this time when we reached the center, I proposed. She said yes!

June 29th, 2019, I led a group of volunteers who came to help complete creating a labyrinth for my hometown of Branford, CT. My suggestion to the town's first selectman a year earlier was immediately embraced. He and the towns crew provided wonderful support in preparing the perfect site. It has been quite remarkable to see my idea become a reality.

Needless to say, labyrinths have indeed changed my life...

It is my hope that creating this book series will bring more people to discover the many wonderful labyrinths available to them in their own states. With luck you will also discover the love, joy and peace I have found.

WJL
Spring 2020

# About Labyrinths

There is not one clear history to be told about labyrinths. They have been around for thousands of years in various forms. They have developed independently in different societies and cultures around the world. Some of the earliest were painted on walls of caves. The term labyrinth is loosely used to differentiate a single path labyrinth from a maze labyrinth. Maze designs are puzzles with many dead ends to keep you from finding the right path to reach the center. While a unicursal labyrinth has but one pathway to the center, and it may have many turns, it will always lead you to the center. Thus, we are reminded to trust the path we are on in our life. Through the years labyrinths have been pagan, decorative, spiritual, and/or religious. In Medieval times they were used as a form of penance and as an alternative form of pilgrimage.

Labyrinths have been enjoying a renaissance which began just before the turn of this century with Lauren Artress, Founder of Veriditas leading the way. The oldest permanent outdoor labyrinth in Connecticut will be found in Litchfield, at Wisdom House, built in 1996. The increased interest in spiritualty and mindfulness seems to have inspired the growth. They can be viewed as a metaphor for life with twists and turns. They teach us to trust that the path we are on is our life's path. Most labyrinths have been built in association with churches, a few private, some municipal and a growing number at hospitals' and other care facilities. People have reported being helped with a wide variety of issues as the result of walking a labyrinth.

The shapes and patterns of labyrinths vary from a simple spiral to the classic Chartres pattern. Materials can vary greatly too. You will find them created with canned food, feathers, rocks, paint, wood, etc. Some are painted on walls or floors others on canvas to provide a portable labyrinth to share. Finger labyrinths are available, made from a wide variety of materials.

# Using this book

You will find a map of Connecticut inside the front cover and one of Rhode Island inside the back cover. Each map has numbered marks showing the location of each labyrinth. The number references the text and photo sequence in the section of the book for that state. We have provided space at the end of each listing for you to make notes as you wish about the labyrinth or your experience.

# CONNECTICUT

# Branford Labyrinth

Shoreline Greenway Trail
62 Tabor Drive, Branford, CT 06405

The labyrinth was originally conceived as a gift to the community as a tool to help resolve the grief following the tragic death of a local youth. At the time the town's Ecology Park seemed the most appropriate location. However, the paving of the section of The Shoreline Greenway Trail, between Tabor Drive and Pine Orchard Road, created access to an even better site overlooking Chet's Pond.

The pattern is a hybrid of the Classical and the Chartres designs with seven rather than 11 circuits. It is called The Circle of Peace™ and was designed by Lisa Gidlow Moriarty. The decision to make the pathways wide enough to accommodate wheelchairs was inspired both by the beautiful labyrinth in West Hartford at the Holy Family Retreat Center in West Hartford, and the accessibility of this section of the Trail.

Town officials were very helpful in supporting the project and worked to prepare the space alongside the trail just for the labyrinth.

First selectman, Jamie Cosgrove, suggested the location and embraced the idea from the start. Gary Zielinski and his crew did a superb job of preparing the site. Special thanks to The Stony Creek Quarry for generously providing all the material to construct the labyrinth.

The Branford Labyrinth was completed June 29th, 2019 with the help of few friends and neighbors in time for the celebration of the town's 375th Anniversary.

Parking is provided at both ends of the trail. One lot is located just off Tabor Drive at the intersection of Ark Road, and the other off Pine Orchard Road just south of the railroad bridge. Follow the paved Shoreline Trail to Chet's Pond. The labyrinth is on the south side of the Trail.

**CONTACT:**

Bill Ludwig
bill@hotchkisspublishing.com
www.hotchkisspublishing.com

or

Branford Parks and Recreation
Branford Community House
46 Church St (Mailing: 1019 Main St)
Branford, CT 06405
recreation@branford-ct.gov
203.488.8304

NOTES:

# Congregational Church of Brookfield

## 160 Whisconier Road, Brookfield, CT 06804

In 2010-2011, the Congregational Church of Brookfield's Confirmation class went to the CT Conference Camp - Silver Lake Conference Center in Sharon, CT for a retreat. While there, they were introduced to the spiritual practice of walking a labyrinth. The Class fell in love with the labyrinth, and the idea of having one closer to home was born.

After returning from the retreat, they approached church leadership about making one on the grounds. There were several unusual or hidden spaces (i.e., an outdoor chapel, a Memorial Garden, campfire circle, refugee cottage, and a barn) to choose from, but the class chose a space that was outlined by trees as the proposed location for the labyrinth. It sits beyond the campfire circle directly behind the cottage used for the Refugee Resettlement Ministry. (Unfortunately, the May 2018 Macroburst that hit the area managed to cause damage to some of the trees, and some had to be cut down.)

The class went through all of the design and proposal phases with the help of some adult mentors, and the project was approved. They reached out to landscapers in the congregation for advice about the materials and procured rocks to outline the labyrinth edges and paths. They held a "You Rock" night where members of the congregation could paint rocks in any way they wished. As a result, the labyrinth has some plain rocks, some rocks that are painted with designs, and others with quotes. The youth fellowship groups came together to lay out the labyrinth and be the first to walk it before the stone dust was delivered. Since the original project was completed there have been some additions - an instruction board built by one of the Senior Youth Fellowship mission teams, and a cross with a Ben's Bell which now adorns the center of the labyrinth that was made as a confirmation project.

The labyrinth is used by members of the local community, by members of the church who are seeking discernment, and by the youth groups and church school children as part of a curriculum focusing on prayer and spiritual practice in their lives. All are welcome during daylight hours.

Park in the generous church parking lot between the upper and lower lots nearest the woods to the south. Follow the garden path southward to the labyrinth. (For large groups, please alert the church office of your plans to walk the labyrinth.)

**CONTACT:**

Jennifer Whipple
203.775.1259 ext.308
jennifer@uccb.org

or

Church Office at office@uccb.org
www.uccb.org

# Essex Elementary School

108 Main Street, Centerbrook, CT  06409

No Photo

This labyrinth is scheduled for completion during the spring of 2020. The project was conceived years ago by the school's environmental group, known as the Green Team. Their goal was to repurpose a paved area once used as tennis courts, but had since become an eyesore and wasted space. The team's idea was to create something of value that would contribute to, and build community. They felt the labyrinth could provide a place for students and staff to use as a resource for reflection, contemplation, and self-regulation, all in an outdoor environment.

The Green Team applied for a grant from The Essex Foundation, a nonprofit corporation dedicated to making a difference in the lives of local citizens by providing and supporting medical, educational, cultural, recreational, and social initiatives. Through their generosity, the team has been able to purchase the supplies needed to bring the project to completion. The labyrinth, a 42-foot Chartres Replica™ made from a stencil set supplied by The Labyrinth Company, is being created by 5th and 6th grade students who are past and present Green Team members.

The labyrinth will be available for public use at no cost during non-school hours only (after 3:30 weekdays, as well as on holidays and weekends). It is located toward the rear of the school building, near the play-scape.

# Guest House Retreat & Conference Center

## 318 West Main Street, Chester, CT 06412

*Photo Credit: Charlie Schillberg*

This lovely 28-foot diameter Abington™ garden labyrinth was built by Guest House staff during the summer of 2012 using a template designed by The Labyrinth Company. It features stone dust pathways that are offset and lined by red brick. The Conference Center's goal in constructing the labyrinth was to provide a way to support their guest's transformational work. It has been used for simple walking meditations, elaborate ceremonies, and rituals.

The labyrinth is available at any time for guests attending meetings or on retreat at the Center. Call or visit the website for additional information.

**CONTACT:**

Guest House Retreat & Conference Center
860.322.5770
www.GuestHouseCenter.org

**NOTES:**

_____

_____

_____

_____

_____

_____

_____

_____

_____

_____

_____

_____

_____

_____

_____

_____

_____

_____

# King Street United Church of Christ

## 201 King Street, Danbury, CT 06811

As with several labyrinths in Connecticut, the pastor of the King Street Church was inspired during a visit to Wisdom House in Litchfield and experienced their labyrinth. She shared this memory: "I walked their labyrinth, and I was praying about my congregation there at King Street. We had recently done an exercise as a congregation that revealed to me how tired they were—some were torn between caring for their aging parents and young children, others tired from years of volunteering in leadership roles, some just from the busyness of life. I thought, 'What can I give them to help them find rest for their souls?' And the thought became obvious: you're walking a labyrinth to find rest for your soul, so why not do the same for them?"

Funds were donated to create this Memorial Labyrinth, and the pastor and church members contributed all the labor to cut and lay the bricks. A Boy Scout also helped with landscaping, part of his Eagle Merit Badge project.

Nestled on a knoll at the northwestern edge of the parking lot away from the churchyard and partially surrounded by woods, it is a peaceful location in spite of the lightly traveled nearby roadway. Nicely maintained, the 31-foot diameter, seven-circuit labyrinth is styled after the one at Wisdom House, with the grass paths which are comfortable underfoot and easy to follow.

**CONTACT:**

KSUCC Church Office
203.748.0719
unitedchurch@sbcglobal.net
http://www.kingstchurch.org

**NOTES:**

# St Stephen's Episcopal Church

## 31 Main Street, East Haddam, CT 06423

St Stephen's is located in the picturesque town of East Haddam with roots going back to 1791. The beautiful English Country Gothic stone church is worthy of a visit in its own right. Attached to the church is the Parish Hall where an octagonal, seven-circuit labyrinth was installed during a remodeling effort which began in 2005.

When the worn and stained carpet in the room was removed, it revealed floor tiles which were suspected of containing asbestos. Rather than disturb the tiles, it was decided that the best course of action would be to install a new wood floor directly over the old one. As the discussion turned to the new flooring pattern, the idea for a labyrinth was suggested by parishioner Liz Johnson. She designed the labyrinth and made a full-scale pattern for the flooring installers to follow.

The Sunday school hosts an annual labyrinth event. The labyrinth also served as an inspiration for the church's new logo pictured above.

The common room is used for a variety of functions. Call the office to inquire about its availability.

**CONTACT:**

Church Office
860.873.9547
office@ststeves.org
www.ststeves.org

**NOTES:**

_____

_____

_____

_____

_____

_____

_____

_____

_____

_____

_____

_____

_____

_____

_____

_____

_____

# EarthenStone Labyrinth

One World Wellness
967 North High Street, East Haven, CT 06512

Founded in 2015, One World Wellness is a holistic center which offers classes in a Taoist yoga and meditation practice called Sundo, as well as other types of healing workshops and wellness events. From this practice, came the inspiration for a labyrinth to provide a place for meditative walking as an alternative to sitting meditation.

EarthenStone Labyrinth at One World Wellness has a single maze-like path with an entrance and an exit. In place of the traditional center circle, this path leads to a circle of log seats with a fire pit in the middle. It was built inside an old cow barn foundation that was part of a dairy farm in the 1920s. Throughout the foundation area you will discover, as you walk, a number of interesting artifacts as well as mythological symbols.

Measuring 25 x 60 feet, the labyrinth, and fire pit area are surrounded by both private landscaped gardens and forest.

Please contact the One World Wellness by phone or email to arrange your visit.

**CONTACT:**

Christine Ucich
203.998.5688
info@oneworld-wellness.com
www.oneworld-wellness.com

**NOTES:**

# Ellington Congregational Church

## 72 Main Street, Ellington, CT 06029

The garden and labyrinth were established in 2008 to commemorate the 275th anniversary of the Ellington Congregational Church. They were funded by contributions to a Memorial Fund and the sale of engraved Memorial River Rocks which form the outer circle of the classical three circuit labyrinth.

In 2015 a cell-antenna was installed in the church steeple and a cable was laid underground throughout the garden. With this project came the opportunity to redesign the labyrinth to accommodate handicap accessibility. The garden was enhanced with a paver entrance continuing with a stone dust path winding through the garden and forming the walkway to journey's end, the labyrinth. The *Pathway to Peace* passes flowering trees, an outdoor classroom, flower-filled pots, and a peaceful fountain, with opportunities to sit and meditate.

Park in the church lot and follow the walkway around the west side of the church to the memorial garden which is easily accessible and always open.

**CONTACT:**

Church Secretary
860.871.6606
eccucc@sbcglobal.net

**NOTES:**

---

---

---

---

---

---

---

---

---

---

---

---

---

# Holy Trinity Episcopal Church

383 Hazard Avenue (Rt. 190), Enfield, CT 06083

This labyrinth of the Holy Trinity Episcopal Church was constructed as an Eagle Scout project by church member, Dan Cushing, and his team of volunteers. Inscribed bricks represent donations by parishioners. The labyrinth was dedicated on November 17, 2013.

You will find a posted information sheet with a guide to using a Prayer Labyrinth, but if it is not available you may ask at the church office. The church requests that while children are most welcome to walk the labyrinth, they should be supervised. Children who prefer a playground will find one next door, west of the church building.

Drive through the church parking lot and park in the upper lot near the parish house. The labyrinth is located at the top of the rise behind the church. The shaded location is relaxing with benches available on either side of the entrance for reflection. It is available to anyone during daylight hours.

**CONTACT:**

Church Secretary
860.749.2722
holy.trinity1@sbcglobal.net
http://www.holytrinityenfield.org

**NOTES:**

# Barker Labyrinth
# @ Purple Door Gallery

13 Bartholomew Hill Road, Goshen, CT 06756

This labyrinth was created in 2004, after a chance meeting between the owner, Lori Barker, and a gentleman named Joe Miguez, who mentioned that his sometime "job" was laying out Labyrinths. He readily agreed to help create one at the Purple Door Gallery. They agreed that it should be located in the woods behind the house and that it would be most natural weaving it through the woods. Lori and her husband, Ernie, walked the site with divining rods and marked three spots of strong energy. Joe was so excited about the location that he immediately went out and marked the pathways with little red flags even though twilight was approaching. He finished in the dark.

The labyrinth paths are lined with chunks of limestone that weave around trees and obstructions. The result, after moving four tons of rocks, is a very pleasing undulating walk. The design is seed-styled, 40 feet in diameter, with seven circuits.

When visiting, ask about the nearby "Touch House" built from straw bales, for further meditation. On New Year's Day, they host a "reading of wishes for the coming year" with a pot-luck lunch following.

Hidden in the woods behind the home and gallery, this labyrinth presents a fascinating walk. Please contact owners to schedule your visit.

### CONTACT:

Lori and Ernie Barker
860.491.3514
lbarker2@optonline.net
http://www.spiritcollage.com

**NOTES:**

_____

_____

_____

_____

_____

_____

_____

_____

_____

_____

# S.O.U.L. Center

## 14 Spring Glen Drive, Granby, CT 06035

This labyrinth was constructed in 2005 following the visit by a local healer. He confirmed that the area to the right of the driveway had strong energy and would be a perfect site for a labyrinth which the owner had dreamed of building. There are 11 circuits, each three feet wide. At 84 feet in diameter, this is the largest labyrinth on private land in Connecticut.

The setting is lovely and convenient with the labyrinth situated in view of a lightly traveled road. An arched trellis welcomes you as you enter the labyrinth. While at first, it appears to be similar to the classic design pattern of Chartres, this labyrinth is a Roman design, and is walked one quadrant at a time. The center offers benches to rest and reflect.

The labyrinth is open to the public during daylight hours. Please contact the owner for availability and to learn about special events.

**CONTACT:**

Tina Angeli
860.653.3612
cangeli@cox.net
http://www.areangels.net

**NOTES:**

# St. Andrews Presbyterian Church

## 310 Fort Hill Road, Groton, CT 06340

Rev. Mark Porizky was inspired to bring a labyrinth to St. Andrews Presbyterian Church in the hopes that "it would draw people back who were looking for spirituality. It's very much intended to be a community gift." Thus, in 2004, he and two dozen volunteers set to work to create this Cretan design, eight circuit labyrinth, with stone dust and fieldstones. The result is a 50-foot diameter labyrinth which fits naturally in its surroundings nestled up to an old stone wall.

It is located in a wooded area between the parking lot and Route 1, but as is often the case, any road noises soon fade away while walking the labyrinth. Upon reaching the center you will find a granite bench welcoming you to rest and reflect.

The funding for this project was provided by the Glass Family Trust in memory of Jerrold Glass.

All are welcome to visit during daylight hours.

**CONTACT:**

Church Secretary
860.445.8848
office@sapc-ct.org
http://sapc-ct.org

**NOTES:**

# Asylum Hill Congregational Church

814 Asylum Avenue, Hartford, CT 06105

In 2001, the church began looking into creating and installing a Meditation Labyrinth on its grounds. Initial plans called for installation outside as part of the landscaping around a new building. However, as final plans came together, it became obvious that enough outdoor space would not be available – so plans moved inside.

It was determined that it would be possible to "resurrect" the original Assembly Room of the church, built in 1903. This area had been closed in and broken into classrooms and offices back in 1938. After it was determined that no significant structural changes were made in 1938, plans were finalized to restore the space to its original scale.

Other than the sanctuary, this would now be the second largest interior space in the church, making it the best location for a labyrinth. Members visited other labyrinths in the region collecting information. They also searched the internet and other sources in hopes of coming up with a design that would fit this new space.

Ultimately, a visit to Village Church in Wellesley, MA and the labyrinth installed in their historic chapel confirmed that this was the right design. The original artist, Robert Ferre in St Louis, MO, was contacted and asked for his assistance. He provided a CAD design for a Chartres-styled seven-circuit 24-foot diameter labyrinth.

Bill Poole, chair of the Board of Worship and Fine Arts, contacted Gerber Scientific for suggestions on template materials and application. The customer service-rep he contacted, Floyd Higgins, was also a musician at a local church. Floyd was so inspired by the project that he made arrangements for Gerber Scientific to provide all technical support for free and even volunteered himself to assist with installation.

In August of 2005, the wood floor was installed in the restored McKeith Hall, and the labyrinth team was given ten days to install the painted labyrinth over the new floor. Floyd Higgins and his wife Gretchen spent nearly 23 hours installing the vinyl adhesive template to the floor in anticipation of the arrival of the volunteer painting crew. Over the next few days, teams of painters from the Board of Worship and Fine Arts, the Choir, and other church artists spent many hours on their knees and stomachs painting, scraping, cleaning and loving this labyrinth into existence. Upon completion, the entire floor was sealed with three additional coats of polyurethane to protect the image.

Please call or email to schedule your visit.

**CONTACT:**

Jack A. Pott, Director of Music & Arts
860.525.5696
jpott@ahcc.org
www.ahcc.org

**NOTES:**

_____

_____

_____

_____

_____

_____

_____

_____

_____

_____

_____

_____

_____

_____

# Hartford Seminary

76 Sherman Street, Hartford, CT 06105

The labyrinth at Hartford Seminary is a classical design with seven circuits and measures 40 feet in diameter.

The labyrinth was a gift from the Women's Leadership Institute alumni and friends of the Medical Mission Sisters. Graduate student Jeanne Pedane designed and constructed it with help from her son Hunter and graduate student Charles Dionne. M & S Paving and Sealing, Inc. of South Windsor, donated the bricks.

The labyrinth was built in memory of Sister Mary Elizabeth Johnson, who lived for 35 years in the house that overlooks the labyrinth grove. She died in May 2014 at the age of 90.

It is easy to find, and is available during daylight hours. The parking area is next to 76 Sherman Street, and the labyrinth is located behind the building in a quiet space bordered by woods; the setting is inviting.

**CONTACT:**

Susan Schoenberger
860.509.9519
sschoenberger@hartsem.edu
https://www.hartsem.edu

**NOTES:**

_____

_____

_____

_____

_____

_____

_____

_____

_____

_____

_____

_____

_____

_____

_____

# Trinity Episcopal Church

120 Sigourney Street, Hartford, CT 06015

The labyrinth at Trinity Church, Hartford, Connecticut, is part of the Trinity Memorial Garden, which was completed in 2001. The garden was designed to create a tranquil oasis amid Trinity's busy urban setting. High brick walls, specimen trees, flowering plants and shrubs, and a gurgling fountain contribute to the atmosphere of this retreat. Cremated remains of parishioners have a resting place in a raised bed against the side of Trinity's large Gothic Revival sanctuary. The garden is not only a refuge for mourners who come to remember their loved ones, but a site where all can find peace and refreshment.

Making the labyrinth a prominent part of the Memorial Garden was the idea of the project's manager, Bill Hamilton. He proposed that the labyrinth's 50-foot wide pavement would provide a useful surface for outdoor worship services and other community events, as well as providing a place for the ancient spiritual exercise of walking the labyrinth's winding paths. It is also fitting that the

Memorial Garden with its labyrinth has become the setting for the lighting of the new fire of Easter.

Once inside the gate of the walled garden area, it is very peaceful. The lines of the labyrinth were recently repainted, enhancing its beauty and utility.

The Trinity labyrinth was designed on-site by Marty Cain. She has created over seventy-five permanent labyrinths throughout America, Canada, and Scotland.

The garden is open on Monday - Thursday from 9:00 am to 3:00 pm from June through September, weather permitting.

**CONTACT:**

Church Secretary
860.527.8133
office@trinityhartford.org
http://www.trinityhartford.org

**NOTES:**

_____

_____

_____

_____

_____

_____

_____

# 16

# St. James Episcopal Church

501 Killingworth Road, Higganum, CT 06441

The Jean Minkler Memorial Labyrinth was designed and built in 2006 by parishioner Howie Burr and three friends from the Higganum community, in memory of a beloved parishioner of St. James.

The Labyrinth is a Classical seven-circuit, 50 feet in diameter design which meanders through the trees. It is rustic, located across the street from the church, nestled behind the Parish Hall in a tranquil woodland setting. It is a magical walk as the paths weave among the trees.

Each year, Easter Sunrise Services are held in the Labyrinth.

The church has plans to make the Labyrinth a memorial space. They hope to have memorial bricks donated by anyone who wants their loved ones remembered.

No need to call ahead. All are invited to enjoy the space and find peace while walking. The Labyrinth is always open, and it is free.

Park across Route 81 (Killingworth Road) from the Church in the lot of the parish hall. You will locate the labyrinth in the woods by following the path in the southwest corner behind the parish hall.

**CONTACT:**

Church Secretary
860.345.2445
wecluster@sbcglobal.net
http://www.stjameshigganum.org

NOTES:

_____

_____

_____

_____

_____

_____

_____

_____

_____

_____

_____

_____

_____

# 17

# Incarnation Camp and
# Conference Center

253 Bushy Hill Road, Ivoryton, CT 06442

Incarnation Center is the oldest continually operating camp in the country, founded in 1886 as a year-round Episcopal camp, retreat, and nature center. Their mission is to provide guests and the public with sacred spaces where they can experience growth, discovery, and renewal. The 740-acre campus provides this in many ways. One of the ways is by providing dedicated spiritual spaces, such as their two chapels or their labyrinth.

The classical 40-foot wide five-circuit labyrinth is located on a hillside pasture bordered by a split rail fence, providing a beautiful, tranquil setting — a perfect labyrinth-site. Visitors may be surprised to discover Incarnation Center, a well-kept secret in the middle of the state.

The Center is open to the public from September through May. In addition to the labyrinth, be sure to check out their miles of hiking trails, farm, and Bushy Hill Nature Center. During the summer months, they host summer camps and a variety of activities, so be sure to contact the office in advance to arrange your visit. Directions to the labyrinth site can be obtained at the office when arriving, as it is located near the center of this large property. Also, ask about the information booklet they offer to aid you during your visit and labyrinth walk.

### CONTACT:

Rev. Dana Stivers
860.767.0848
dstivers@incarnationcenter.org
https://www.incarnationcenter.org

**NOTES:**

# 18

# Congregational Church of Killingworth, UCC

273 Route 81, Killingworth, CT 06419

This seven-circuit, classical, 45-foot labyrinth was built in the spring of 2004 by a long-time Killingworth resident, Bill Jette. Hand-placing the 1,353 small stones which comprise the seven circuits took about 100 hours to complete.

The builder liked to say that "Life is not a straight path, so, therefore, the labyrinth is not a straight path. There are obstacles along the way because life has obstacles." In keeping with that thought, this labyrinth weaves its way through the woods with a tree in the middle of one circuit.

A 500lb boulder was hand-rolled out of the church woods to its current location at the entrance to the labyrinth. It holds a plaque dedicating the labyrinth to those interred in the nearby Memorial Garden.

To find your way to the labyrinth, park in the lot on the south side of the church. Walk to the back of the yard (southeast corner) and follow the sign for the Memorial Garden. Just after the outdoor chapel, you will notice the labyrinth on the left. If there are many leaves on the ground, it may take a little searching as the labyrinth naturally blends into the woods. It is a joy to walk. Everyone is welcome to visit during daylight hours. For large groups, please call the church office.

**CONTACT:**

Church Secretary, Maureen Alfiero
860.663.1789
office@killingworthchurch.com
http://www.killingworthchurch.com

**NOTES:**

# 19

# Someday Farm

272 Roast Meat Hill Road, Killingworth, CT 06419

The Someday Farm is a unique property that is difficult to describe. The current owner, Stephen Watson, provides horse boarding, training in Chinese Arts, and much more. Stephen eloquently stated that this is "where horses live happily, Native people sought solace, and people come to learn to be their better selves."

Greg Coleman, created a 40-foot diameter labyrinth for the previous owner. It is situated overlooking the pond, which makes it a more a tranquil setting. The pathways are defined by rocks, brick, etc. which are somewhat buried in places making them difficult at times to follow. This has the beneficial effect of forcing one to be present and focus on the path. Stephen has done a good deal of work to restore the labyrinth and uncover the pathways. Visiting here will be a worthwhile experience and time well spent. Perhaps the opportunity will present itself to see the beavers working on their den in the pond.

An advance call to your host, Stephen is appreciated. He is sure to provide a very warm welcome.

**CONTACT:**

Stephen Watson
farmingoursomedays@gmail.com
https://www.facebook.com/SomedayFarmLLC

**NOTES:**

_____

_____

_____

_____

_____

_____

_____

_____

_____

_____

_____

_____

_____

# 20

# Wisdom House

## 229 E Litchfield Rd, Litchfield, CT 06759

The Wisdom House Retreat and Conference Center was founded in 1949 by the Daughters of Wisdom. This labyrinth is thought to be the first outdoor labyrinth in Connecticut. It was originally conceived in 1991 to provide a universal tool to help encourage greater spirituality. Barbara Putman designed it, and the construction was undertaken in 1996 by volunteers. It was dedicated on June 8, 1997.

One has only to stroll down a grassy hillside to the level garden space below containing this elegantly simple labyrinth. It was constructed with only bricks and rocks forming the borders of the circuits and grass on the pathways, which makes for a comfortable walking surface, with or without shoes. The simple seven-circuit Cretan design circles back and forth until you reach the center without any unnecessary twists or turns.

This wonderful labyrinth has spawned and inspired many of the other labyrinths found throughout the state. It is available during daylight hours, and a suggested donation is welcome to help keep it maintained.

**CONTACT:**

Deborah Kelly
Tel: 860.567.3163
deborah@wisdomhouse.org
www.wisdomhouse.org

**NOTES:**

_____

_____

_____

_____

_____

_____

_____

_____

_____

_____

_____

_____

_____

# 21

# Hammonasset State Park

1288 Boston Post Road, Madison, CT 06443

This Park area was named Hammonasset by the tribe of Eastern Woodland Indians. The word Hammonasset means where we dig holes in the ground- a reference to the tribe's agricultural way of life. In 1919, the lands that would comprise the Park were acquired and on July 18, 1920, Hammonasset Beach State Park was opened to the public. Today, the only holes being dug are on the beach by children.

No one is certain when the first stones were laid to begin the spiral, which is now the Labyrinth at Hammonasset. The best guess is that it began around 2014, and has grown each year as visitors have added rocks, shells, and logs to extend the spiral design. It has now reached the tideline preventing further expansion. Instead, visitors have been adding to the rock pile in the center. This spiral labyrinth might best be described as "spontaneous" in design. It is more than 80' in diameter but it is very dynamic and subject to change due to storms etc.

Park visitors should follow the road signs in the direction of Meigs Point Nature Center then continue past to the road's end at Hammonasset Point parking. From the parking lot walk the path east to the shell beach. The labyrinth will be "discovered" at the far end.

NOTE: Only campers and fishers with passes may enter the park after sunset. In the off-season, the gates are unlocked at 8:00 am and are locked at sunset. Check the park website for details.

**CONTACT:**

Park Office 203.245.2785
https://www.ct.gov/deep/site/


or

Meigs Point Nature Center
203.245.8743
www.meigspointnaturecenter.org


**NOTES:**

# 22

# Mercy by the Sea Retreat and Conference Center

167 Neck Road, Madison, CT 06643

Mercy by the Sea's labyrinth is a left-handed seven-circuit labyrinth located on the western end of their beachfront with spectacular views of Long Island Sound. It is constructed of brick, boxwood and Stony Creek granite. The brick and boxwood provide the borders for the stone path. Conceived by Sr. Genie Guterch, RSM, and constructed by Ted Ozyck, it was opened in 1998. In 2014, it was refurbished as an Eagle Scout Service Project.

Weather permitting, Mercy by the Sea offers monthly full moon labyrinth walks which are open to the public, registration is required. According to the Center, "These are opportunities to be still and aware of God's presence within us and all around us. To prepare for the walk, participants gather first for prayer in Lyons Chapel. The prayer is focused on our desire for peace in our hearts and the world. It enables us to ready our hearts and to let go of any anxiety we may be holding in our bodies so that we are fully prepared to receive the gift intended for us while walking the labyrinth and in particular from the time spent in the center of the labyrinth."

Each of the full moon labyrinth walks conclude with a comfortable cup of tea and sharing about what was felt, seen, and heard during the walk.

Mercy by the Sea is located on Neck Road in Madison, CT. It is approximately two miles off the Post Road. Make a left-hand turn when you see its sign and proceed down the road to the retreat center where you will need to check-in. Follow the aroma of salt water toward Long Island Sound to find this lovely, three-dimensional labyrinth.

Note: This labyrinth can be a bit confusing at the start. Be sure to follow the stone path rather than the bricks.

**CONTACT:**

Ann McGovern, RSM
203.245.0401
amcgovern@mercyne.org
https://www.mercybythesea.org/campus/labyrinth

**NOTES:**

_____

_____

_____

_____

_____

# 23

# Immanuel Evangelical Lutheran Church

## 164 Hanover Street, Meriden, CT 06451

In November of 1999, as the result of reading an article about labyrinths in *The Lutheran* magazine, parishioner Blair Goodlin was led to several labyrinth related events. During one weekend event, he recalled asking himself, "Basically, what am I doing here? What am I doing here? It dawned on me. I was there to bring the medieval labyrinth to Immanuel Church. That was why I was there."

His research led him to select a Maltese design for the labyrinth, which is octagonal. He determined it would be the simplest to lay-out, not needing a tape measure or special tools. Using only the 12-inch floor tiles, he was able to create a labyrinth 28 tiles wide and 28 high with 11 circuits. In September 2002, he and some members of the congregation laid out blue masking tape on the floor and painted the 1-inch borders.

When they were finished and took up the tape, they looked at the finished labyrinth and concluded, "Well, how very Lutheran. Because in Lutheran theology, we are all both saints and sinners, and here we have a labyrinth the lines and walls for which are both perfect and imperfect." When being painted the walls were bound by tape on only one side, so the tape side is "perfectly" straight, while the free side shows the fluctuations in the pressure on the 1-inch foam paintbrush, i.e., is "imperfect."

Since this space is used for different functions, please call the office to arrange a suitable time to visit and walk the labyrinth.

### CONTACT:

Church Office
203.238.1248
Monday-Friday 9am-1pm
office@immanuelmeriden.org
http://immanuelmeriden.org

NOTES:
_____

_____

_____

_____

_____

_____

_____

# 24

# Unitarian Universalist Church

328 Paddock Avenue, Meriden, CT 06450

This unique labyrinth, The Spiral Garden, is a special place of beauty located behind Unitarian Universalist Church in Meriden. The garden is based on one that was once in Middletown, CT, created by the spiritual director and environmentalist, Eleanore Milardo. Her garden was recognized by the Smithsonian Institute's Landscape Garden Division for innovation and naturalness.

After her death, the signs in the garden were left to her good friend, Diane Szymaszek, who was inspired to recreate it behind Unitarian Universalist Church in Meriden with the help of friends and a few students. It is in a spiral shape and is inhabited by mostly native plants. The signs along the path tell the story of the Universe and our connection to all life. This garden provides a wonderful place where one can walk the spiral and sit and find peace in this busy world.

Park in the church's parking lot and follow the walkway which leads to the rear of the church. The spiral is straight across the lawn.

**CONTACT:**

Office Administrator
203.237.9297
http://uucentralct.org

**NOTES:**

_____

_____

_____

_____

_____

_____

_____

_____

_____

_____

_____

_____

_____

_____

_____

_____

# 25

# Wesleyan University

## 45 Wyllys Avenue, Middletown CT 06459

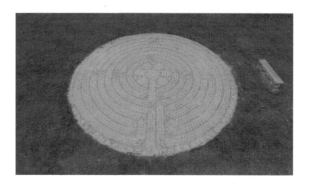

*Photo Credit: Patrick Bohan*

The Wesleyan University Labyrinth, which was created in 2009, is easily accessible to all campus visitors and can be found near the corner of Wyllys and Davis streets. The pattern is a copy of the Chartres Cathedral labyrinth constructed with colored concrete pavers. (credit: Labyrinth Company, Vision Quest à la Chartres™ paver kit)

It is located between the Skull and Serpent building and the Davison Art Center Courtyard; the 30-foot-wide seven circuit labyrinth is the result of six years of planning and alumni fundraising. The labyrinth was presented to Wesleyan to honor Kit and Joe Reed. Kit was an author and resident writer at Wesleyan, and Joe was a professor emeritus of English and American Studies who taught film courses at Wesleyan from the mid-1960s until his retirement in 2004.

"Every university should have a labyrinth, for it represents our desire to unravel the essential mysteries of human existence. It is a problem to be solved, a question to be answered, and a paradox to be considered. Each labyrinth has a center and, as a diagram of learning, its tangled patterns lead us to that hidden core. Even as the pursuit of knowledge follows many diverging paths, there is also a basic symmetry to these designs, a unified whole that pleases the eye and piques the mind." -Stephen Alter '77

**CONTACT:**

Marcy Herlihy
860.685.2523
mherlihy@wesleyan.edu
www.wesleyan.edu

**NOTES:**

_____

_____

_____

_____

_____

_____

_____

_____

_____

_____

_____

# 26

# Yale Divinity School

## 409 Prospect Street, New Haven, CT 06511

The 2002 remodeling of the Divinity School markedly changed the nature of the Sterling Quadrangle. It was the end of residential occupancy on the quad leaving the Chapel, administrative offices, classrooms and faculty offices.

The most recent remodeling of the Georgian-style complex has included the two long-neglected outside courtyard areas at the east end of the buildings. The northeast side provides a courtyard to be used by the public for outdoor receptions, the serving of meals, enjoy a remarkable gas pit, or a place for people to sit and relax.

The southeast courtyard has been designated quiet space for students, faculty, and staff to sit and reflect. It is also a perfect spot to add a labyrinth as an invitation to think about life and our relationship with God. Hence, a labyrinth of the Chartres design was created due to all these appealing features that it possessed. (credit: Labyrinth Company, Vision Quest à la Chartres™ paver kit)

Its proximity to the church is representative of movement toward communion with God. One enters the labyrinth in contemplation of life and relationship to the Divine, moving toward its center which symbolizes God. This stunning labyrinth will provide the perfect setting for all who desire this experience.

Park your vehicles at the designated spots and follow the driveway to the rear of the building where you will see the entrance to the southeast quad where the labyrinth is located.

**CONTACT:**

Tom Krattenmaker
203.436.8379
tom.krattenmaker@yale.edu
https://divinity.yale.edu

**NOTES:**

_____

_____

_____

_____

_____

_____

_____

_____

_____

_____

# 27

# Sticks and Stones Farm

## 201 Huntingtown Road, Newtown, CT 06470

The Sticks and Stones Farm is aptly named because, for years, its main crop has been stones. Lots of stones! The property owner, Tim Currier, discovered that there was a market with an insatiable appetite for stones to build stonewalls, rock gardens, and the like. In addition to supplying stones, he grew and sold moss.

Today, this unique Farm offers a variety of stones, mosses for sale, and maintains an organic vegetable garden which supplies their kitchen and farm stand as well as local food banks. Also offered are cabin rentals, yoga, massage, miles of hiking trails, and event hosting.

Tim's former partner, Annie Stiefel, was first smitten with the wonders of labyrinths during a 2000 visit to rural Ireland when she encountered one of the Chartres design. This led to her idea, in 2009, to create one on the farm. Tim cleared an area in the woods just above the Pootatuck River to accommodate what would become a 54-foot labyrinth surrounded by old Belgium Blocks. The 11-circuit pattern duplicates the original Chartres.

Tim and Annie enlisted lots of help to complete the labyrinth in time to host a walking memorial for a young individual who died from a drug overdose. This evolved into a monthly grief group which concluded with a labyrinth walk. The labyrinth continues to attract people, farm guests, neighbors, labyrinth enthusiasts, and others seeking a peaceful place to think and unwind. It is also used for weddings, full-moon walks, and drum circles.

After the Sandy Hook shooting, Tim and Annie opened the farm's barn and the labyrinth up to all that were affected by the tragedy as a place for healing and solace.

Smoke, drug and alcohol free, the beautiful hiking trails are open from May 1 to October 31st. All visitors are asked to sign a liability form at the stone barn, obtain a map, and leave a donation for trail maintenance. Dogs must be leashed.

**CONTACT:**

Bill Donaldson, Property Steward/Manager
203.915.0718
info@sticksandstonesfarm.com
https://www.sticksandstonesfarm.com

**NOTES:**

_____

_____

_____

_____

_____

_____

# 28

# Trinity Episcopal Church

36 Main St, Newtown, CT 06470

This beautifully executed, 24-foot diameter, six-circuit Chartres-styled labyrinth came to Newtown through the efforts of Jack Benedict, a young Boy Scout and member of Trinity Church. During a youth pilgrimage to the Black Hills of North Dakota, he was inspired by a visit to a beautiful outdoor labyrinth there. Jack felt it would be a great Eagle Scout project, as well as a wonderful gift to his church and town to create something similar.

Designed by The Labyrinth Company (Abingdon à la Chartres™ paver kit), all the materials as well as necessary site preparation work were donated by generous businesses and individuals. Jack recruited 33 volunteers, including Troop 270 leaders and Scouts, adults and youth from Trinity, and his family and friends. The volunteers spent Saturday, June 8, 2013, placing pavers by hand, creating a handicap-accessible pathway, installing an edge restraint, sweeping polymeric sand into the joints, and re-planting grass around the edges.

"I am happy I was able to build such a beautiful labyrinth for my church and community," said Jack. "I am thankful for the major donations that made the project possible, and I enjoyed learning about labyrinth construction and about planning a project."

The labyrinth is near the gazebo at Trinity's Memorial Garden, yet is set apart for spiritual reflection and prayer, offering a highly effective practice for reducing stress and anxiety.

The gazebo and labyrinth are easily found by following the driveway to the right of the church to one of the parking lots. The church welcomes visitors to walk the labyrinth during daylight hours.

### CONTACT:

203.426.9070
admin@trinitynewtownct.org
www.trinitynewtownct.org

**NOTES:**

_____

_____

_____

_____

_____

_____

_____

_____

# 29

# McCook Park Beach

8-10 Atlantic Street, Niantic, CT 06357

While on a retreat, Joanne Moore was introduced to labyrinths, and fully embraced the experience. There, Reverend Lee Ireland presented information on their history, labyrinths as a metaphor, how to set an intention, and walking as meditation.

Five years later following the death of her husband from cancer, Joanne was at The Mercy Center, in Madison, CT. It was a foggy, early morning as she started walking the labyrinth, having set her intention as a search for what the next chapter of her life should be. At the center, she heard a voice that said, "Every seven years let the fields lay fallow," a passage from the Old Testament, indicating the need for rest. Joanne's experience at the labyrinth had followed seven years of caring for her husband. Just then, the fog lifted, revealing the beauty of Long Island Sound, and from that point, she became enamored of labyrinths.

She began building one annually on the beach in Niantic at McCook's Point, using the stones she found there. She would place the stones in early November, then maintain the labyrinth throughout the fall, winter, and spring until Memorial Day when the town would clear the beach for summer use. Depending on the number of stones available, some were modeled after the Chartres design, and others were classic seven-circuit labyrinths. By the end of each walking season, the path would be depressed 6 inches below the level of the stones as evidence of much use.

This suggested the need for a permanent labyrinth. Joanne approached Dave Putnam, Director of Parks and Recreation in East Lyme, who agreed to help build one. Using a backhoe, he smoothed an area, 30-foot circumference, on a grassy knoll and covered it with crushed stones. With help from members of the Niantic Community Church, Joanne laid the stones to create a classic-styled, permanent labyrinth.

From the main vehicle entrance to McCook Park follow the roadway to the second parking area at the top of the hill. There you will see a covered pavilion and an amphitheater. Continue for a short distance past the pavilion and amphitheater to the labyrinth. For fees and park hours consult their website.

**CONTACT:**

Parks & Recreation
860.739.5828
parkinfo@eltownhall.com
https://eltownhall.com/visitors-recreation/sites-of-interest/beaches

**NOTES:**

# 30

# Norwalk Community College

188 Richards Avenue, Norwalk, Connecticut 06854

The Norwalk Community College in Norwalk, Connecticut, is the home of the Annual Goose Feather Labyrinth which is designed, engineered, and constructed by Renae Edge, Professor of Public Speaking and Theater. Renae began constructing the labyrinths in 2010. In each subsequent year, students, faculty, staff, alumni, and community neighbors have helped in the construction. The labyrinths contain between 900 and 1200 primary wing feathers that are annually molted by Canada Geese and collected at a nearby location. Some designs have included turkey or peacock feathers. The theme for each year's labyrinth, built in early autumn, is different and is based on a personal or social issue that resonates deeply with Renae at the time. Often a statement about the theme is posted at the labyrinth. Most designs are variations of a traditional eight-ring, circular pattern, but others have been intertwined spirals, an unimpeded spiral, a center heart that gradually became a circle, concentric hearts, and a wave that crested onto itself.

Construction takes between eight to twelve hours, depending on the complexity of the design. The feathers are held in the ground simply by the compression of the soil and remain in place until they are mowed late the next summer. Crystals are placed in the holes made by the marking stakes as they are removed during the construction, and remain in the earth as tokens of gratitude and to surround the labyrinth walkers with healing energy. The labyrinths are always on the East Campus, at the top of the hill between Richards Avenue and the North parking lot. The opening is at the foot of the evergreen tree in the middle of the hill.

**CONTACT:**

Renae Edge
203.857.7235
REdge@ncc.commnet.edu
https://norwalk.edu

**NOTES:**

_____

_____

_____

_____

_____

_____

_____

_____

_____

_____

_____

# 31

# St. Paul's on the Green

## 60 East Avenue, Norwalk, CT 06851

St. Paul's Church is located, near the center of Norwalk, on a fenced-in "island" comprising an entire city block. Along with the church, the site includes a churchyard and cemetery, as well as a meditation garden and labyrinth that appear almost like an oasis on the church's property.

The stone labyrinth was designed and built in the summer of 2003 by Michael Mushak, as a gift of thanks to the St. Paul's community and the community at large. Michael hand laid approximately 10,000 individual stones on a 12-inch base of gravel. It was constructed in the churchyard which had been under-used and neglected. Located next to the common room, it provides a convenient patio for special events. This labyrinth is a medieval seven-circuit modified Chartres pattern, and 40 feet in diameter, making it a good fit for the space available. The labyrinth was consecrated on Sunday, November 23rd, 2003.

The labyrinth is open to the public and is now the centerpiece of the church's healing garden and outreach ministry, and the setting for many special and memorable events.

Park on the street and follow the walkway through the burial area toward the church entrance. Proceed around the eastern side of the church to the rear where there is a peaceful sitting area and the labyrinth. Both are always available for use.

**CONTACT:**

Marsha Dunn
203.847.2806
info@stpaulsnorwalk.org
www.stpaulsnorwalk.org

**NOTES:**

_____

_____

_____

_____

_____

_____

_____

_____

_____

_____

# 32

# The Church of the Good Shepherd

## 680 Racebrook Road, Orange, CT 06477

This labyrinth was conceived and constructed as an Eagle Scout project in 2013 by Richard Angal, a young church member. He wished to contribute something to the parish which would combine faith & prayer in an outdoor environment. When a labyrinth was suggested, he realized that it was the perfect project which would last for many years.

It was designed as a classical Seed pattern by Richard's uncle Brian DeLorme and built with the help of his family, other Boy Scouts, and church members. Others from the community provided support or donated materials.

The location has the feeling of being more remote than its actual proximity to Racebrook Road would seem to allow. It is thirty-feet in diameter with very comfortable rubber walkways. However, it may prove challenging for those who have difficulty walking or with balance.

Parking is available in either the upper main church parking lot or in the secondary driveway accessed from Pryde Drive. When the church office is open, literature about walking the labyrinth is available.

**CONTACT:**

Church Office:
Church Secretary
203.795.6577
https://www.thegoodshepherdorangect.org
thegoodshepherd@optonline.net

**NOTES:**

_____

_____

_____

_____

_____

_____

_____

_____

_____

_____

# 33

# Open Sky Yoga Barn

## 95 Cross Highway, Redding, CT 06896

Forest labyrinths seem to possess an energy unlike any others, and this one is a prime example. Soon after Cathy Whelehan started Open Sky Yoga Barn in 2011, she had an intuition that there was supposed to be a labyrinth on the property.

The next few years were consumed with running the business as well as forays into labyrinth research.

In time, she found herself dreaming about labyrinths until the energy in the dreams told her to "Just go out there, and we'll show you how to do it." She began working on it with a friend, and they felt guided in locating the labyrinth amongst the trees which she left, only removing dead ones and some saplings that gave their permission. She enlisted others to help as work continued, and they too seemed to be guided as they created the 66' diameter pattern.

Eleven circuits were laid-out into a pattern similar to Chartres design, using stones harvested from the property. The labyrinth was completed in the summer of 2016.

The labyrinth can be found in a wooded area to the left the long driveway just before it emerges into the clearing where the studio and other buildings are. Visitors are welcome during daylight hours and may park in front of the labyrinth.

**CONTACT:**

Catherine Whelehan
203.648.8023
cwheels33@me.com
http://www.openskyyogabarn.com

NOTES:

_____

_____

_____

_____

_____

_____

_____

_____

_____

_____

# 34

# Garden of Ideas

## 653 North Salem Road, Ridgefield, CT 06877

The Garden of Ideas is a most surprising discovery due to its location in the center of Fairfield County where one would expect only private estates. Its 12 acres is home to all sorts of wonders and offers many reasons to visit. There are lovely gardens, both wild and cultivated, as well as several walking paths along which you will find a variety of whimsical sculptures.

One of these paths leads to a remote labyrinth hidden deep in the woods. It was designed by the owner, Joseph Keller, who built it with the help of Diego, Eddison, and Tio Leon. They situated it in a tranquil location where visitors will likely wish to linger (though during summer, bug spray may be needed).

Joseph had wanted to build a labyrinth for a long time. It took the seemingly unconnected donation of an antique greenhouse to set the labyrinth wheels in motion. About halfway through dismantling the greenhouse, the donor wanted to make sure they were also going to remove the four-foot-high concrete foundation as well. The resulting 20 yards of concrete rubble came to provide a firm base for the labyrinth, as well as the impetus to make it a reality.

Vegetable and ornamental plants are available for sale in the spring, as well as intriguing garden objects such as gnomes, gargoyles, Buddhas, and fairy gardens throughout the year.

The web site offers a post summarizing their purpose and philosophy: "We are a 501c-3 non-profit with a mission to maintain and improve our restorative, tranquil, educational garden. We are an analog antidote to a demented digital world."

The labyrinth is available during daylight hours.

**CONTACT:**

Joseph Keller
203.431.9914
one--gardenofideas@outlook.com
https://gardenofideas.com

**NOTES:**

_____

_____

_____

_____

_____

_____

# 35

# The Way of the Labyrinth

## 2 Rose Lane, Stonington, CT 06378

Following the loss of her husband in 2005, Judith Clinton felt that she should do something about the overgrown tennis court on the property which her husband had always imagined repurposing. Seven years passed, during which time she came to learn much about labyrinths and their usefulness.

In 2012, Mother Nature intervened in the form of Hurricane Sandy. The property was a mess with lots of trees down, requiring heavy machinery to clean up.

Since the equipment was there, it was seen as the most expedient way to clear the mess at the tennis court as well. Once cleaned, it presented the perfect opportunity to build a labyrinth in the spot where her late husband had dreamed of having a garden. It would become a place one could visit to meditate and find a sense of peace and calm. After replacing the asphalt with a stone dust base, the excavator moved the many huge stones that (naturally for

Stonington) populated the property. These boulders formed the outer border of the 54-foot diameter labyrinth. The inner paths were lined with many smaller stones to create the 11 circuits following the pattern of the labyrinth in the cathedral in Chartres, France. Seashells decorate the area of demarcation where the pathways turn. The result is a lovely labyrinth in a beautiful, private setting.

To this day, she is sure that the idea for a labyrinth that came out of the blue was a communication from her husband's spirit. Judith has now turned her home and property into an Artist's retreat center, where she also conducts One Day Labyrinth Workshops.

Please contact here to arrange your visit.

**CONTACT:**

Judith Clinton
860.535.0754
Jclinton14@msn.com
http://www.thewayofthelabyrinth.com

**NOTES:**

_____

_____

_____

_____

_____

_____

# 36

# Unicorn Meadow Farm

1349 Spruce Street, Suffield, CT 06078

The right-hand six-circuit design for this 40-foot labyrinth was inspired by a photograph in a book of an old English Church. Nancy Allen and Jackie Lenko chose the North/South orientation "because north is the direction of magic and south is the direction of personal power." The initial construction was in 2013, with bricks laid into the earth because they believed that they would only have to mow the grass to keep it up and because friends had a pallet of bricks they were willing to donate. After a few years of trying to maintain this configuration, they decided to change. They replaced the grass with a base of dirt and sand. Next, friends brought rocks which were placed on top of the bricks to create the labyrinth you see today. Later a trellis was added at the entrance.

The owner tells this sweet story of an older neighbor, a farmer, who stopped to ask about their garden: "He's a retired farmer or semi-retired farmer, and he drives a pickup truck, his flannel shirt sleeves rolled up. He stopped one day, and he says, 'I've been watching that garden. You're not growing anything there. What is it? I'm just curious.' So, I told him what it was, and he comes and walks it now."

It is easy to find the labyrinth conveniently located next to the road. Always available during daylight hours, the owners request visitors to park on the street and please be quiet during your visit.

**CONTACT:**

Nancy Allen
860.668.6424
k9koral@yahoo.com
http://www.unicornmeadowfarm.com

**NOTES:**

_____

_____

_____

_____

_____

_____

_____

_____

_____

_____

# 37

# Rob & Nancy Henderson

521 North Street, Terryville, CT 06786

This lovely labyrinth was inspired by the labyrinth at The Wisdom House Retreat and Conference Center in Litchfield, CT. Similarly, this one features a classic pattern constructed on a grass field with bricks for the walls. The owner recounts her experience walking her first labyrinth at Wisdom House: "As I took my first steps into the labyrinth, I immediately noticed a sense of solitude and thoughtfulness. Although I was exposed to the expanse of the lawn, I felt enclosed and protected. Just before I reached the center, a woman stepped into the labyrinth, and a great rush of energy seemed to spiral ahead of her and flow through me like a gust of warm air. As I arrived at the center, I realized how deeply immersed I was in the simple act of walking, focused on the path, and my meditations. I felt centered."

After visiting other labyrinths and reading several books and internet resources, she realized that she wanted to create her own, personal labyrinth believing that the process of designing and building would deepen her connection and heighten the experience of walking the labyrinth.

In 2000 using only a photo as a guide she began construction. Rather than following traditional building methods, she started with the center open circle outlined with bricks and stone. The paths grew from the center. Many adjustments were made to accommodate the turns and entrance. It has endured many renovations since then and is now embedded in a thick green lawn. It was dedicated on August 11, 2002.

All are welcome, however, please call to arrange a visit.

**CONTACT:**

Nancy & Rob Henderson
860.583.5841
nhenderson@comcast.net

__NOTES:__ _____

_____

_____

_____

_____

_____

_____

_____

_____

# 38

# Quinnipiac River Linear Trail

489 Hall Avenue (RT 150), Wallingford, CT 06492

The Quinnipiac River Linear Trail Advisory Committee had invited AmeriCorps NCCC, the national service organization specializing in conservation, to help improve the trail. The AmeriCorps volunteers came to Connecticut the year following the September 11, 2001 World Trade Center attack. Feeling the need to offer even more to the community than had been asked, they offered to build a labyrinth as a symbol of peace and consolation. The result was the creation of this classic seven-circuit, 40-foot diameter labyrinth made of stone dust and brick.

The labyrinth is just a short walk from the parking lot and located on the right side of the trail. There are two benches provided nearby for rest and reflection.

Take the Wilbur Cross Parkway (Route 15) to Exit 65. Take North Turnpike Road (Route 150) as it curves southwards. The entrance to the Community Lake/Linear Trail parking lot is on the left just after crossing over the Wilbur Cross Parkway. The trail begins next to the park entrance.

**CONTACT:**

Town of Wallingford Parks & Recreation Department
203.294.2120

or

The Quinnipiac River Linear Trail Advisory Committee
203.430.0921 or 203.314.5665

**NOTES:**

_____

_____

_____

_____

_____

_____

_____

_____

_____

_____

_____

_____

_____

_____

# 39

# First Congregational Church

## 6 Kirby Road, Washington, CT 06793

The idea for a permanent labyrinth on the floor of Weresebe Hall in the Parish House of the First Congregational Church U.C.C. in Washington, Connecticut grew out of a group study on the different types of prayer, including centering prayer, chant, meditation on an object, and walking meditation using a labyrinth. Using blue painter's tape to lay out a temporary labyrinth, they used this for meditation and prayer for a couple of weeks. For ease of measurement and layout, the group decided on an octagonal labyrinth that would be all straight lines. The labyrinth at the Amiens Cathedral in Somme, France, and the one at the Reims Cathedral in Reims, France (which now only exists in a manuscript drawing) were created in octagonal form and inspired the Weresebe Hall Labyrinth. To make the path wide enough for two people to pass each other, and with limited floor space of the hall, they planned a 30-foot 6-circuit labyrinth.

In September 2012, the congregation decided to create a permanent labyrinth. However, because at the time, a Nursery School used the hall as a playground when weather conditions forced them inside, painting had to wait until Christmas break. This allowed the paint to dry before the children's return.

The floor is made of maple, which has two distinct shades, so they used two different colors of paint. The darker one was used for the first coat, and a lighter color was applied as the second coat to create the appearance of a grain. Though amateurs at faux finishes, they have managed to fool casual visitors. For the center design, the group chose a compass rose to symbolize God's guidance, always available at the center of our being.

The creators were Rev. Cheryl Anderson, Administrative Assistant Karen Esslinger, and Ellen Willert, a member of the church. The painting was completed after Christmas 2012. The inaugural use of the completed labyrinth was for a special labyrinth meditation program during Lent, 2013.

This space is often used for other purposes, so it is a good idea to call or email the office to arrange your visit. It is typically available Monday through Friday, 9 am to 5 pm and some evenings.

**CONTACT:**

Karen Esslinger
860.868.0569
admin@firstchurchwashingtom.org
www.firstchurchwashington.org

**NOTES:**

# 40

# St. John's Episcopal Church

## 16 Church Street, Waterbury, CT 06702

St John's Church is located in the heart of downtown Waterbury directly across from the town green. The labyrinth is located next to the church in an area they refer to as the "Close." At the time the labyrinth was conceived, this was the area where many who visited the church's soup kitchen would wait for its opening, enjoying the peace of the space. Because this was a quiet but public space, it was perfect for a labyrinth.

The original construction was completed in 2004 by John Burton; a priest experienced in building labyrinths. He had a couple of dozen volunteers to assist. The design is a replica of the labyrinth at the Chartres Cathedral in France with 11 circuits and is 40 feet in diameter. The Soup Kitchen was relocated, and over time, the labyrinth was neglected. In 2017, a group of church members restored the labyrinth to the superb condition it is in today. It is a beautiful gift to the people of this city and worthy of a visit.

Park on Church Street for direct access to the courtyard with the labyrinth.

**CONTACT:**

Parish Administrative Assistant
203.754.3116
http://www.stjohnsonthegreen.org
sthohns@stjohnsonthegreen.org

**NOTES:**

_____

_____

_____

_____

_____

_____

_____

_____

_____

_____

_____

_____

# 41

# First Church of Christ Congregational

## 12 South Main Street, West Hartford, CT 06107

*Left Photo Credit: Mick Melvin*

This 36-foot diameter, Chartres style labyrinth with 11 circuits, is beautifully incorporated into the overall landscape of the public churchyard, and it is located directly on the main thoroughfare in the heart of West Hartford. The story behind its creation follows a similar pattern to many church labyrinth

In late fall of 1999, members from First Church gathered over a weekend in the basement of the church to paint a large canvas labyrinth which had been commissioned. After that, the canvas labyrinth was available once a month for people to walk. The labyrinth was also used for worship experiences at First Church and other churches borrowed it for various retreats and workshops.

Around 2001, the church began plans to update the landscaping in the front of First Church and expanding the Memorial Garden next to the Chapel. It was agreed to include an outdoor labyrinth as a part of the design. Peter Chow, architect and landscape designer, was hired and Francisco Gomes completed building the labyrinth in 2004.

Perhaps one of the most significant experiences on the outdoor labyrinth was during an interfaith service that was held on the evening of September 11, 2011, in honor of the 10th anniversary of 9/11. At the end of the service in the Chapel, each person was given a candle, and processed out to the labyrinth and created a human peace sign. (Please see photo). Christian, Jewish, and Muslim people stood together, honoring the Holy invitation to peace among all. One holocaust survivor who attended with his Rabbi was deeply touched by the experience. He never thought there would be a day he would stand united with Jews, Christians, and Muslims in this fashion.

All are invited to come and walk this labyrinth and have their own experiences.

Parking is available on South Main Street directly in front of the Labyrinth which is located in the courtyard facing the street. Additional parking is in the church's lot accessible from Farmington Avenue located directly behind the Church and parish house.

**CONTACT:**

First Church Office.
860.233.9605
general.mail@whfirstchurch.org

NOTES:

# 42

# Holy Family Retreat Center

## 303 Tuxis Road, West Hartford, CT 06107

The labyrinth at Holy Family Passionist Retreat Center was completed in 2007. It was constructed from local fieldstone and original cobblestones from the first streets of Manhattan. At the center of the labyrinth is a circular sculpture created by stonemason Dan Sieracki. Their website has this to say about labyrinth; "The circle is a symbol of eternity and the fullness of life to which God calls each of us. The circle is simultaneously a reminder of emptiness inviting us to empty ourselves so that we might be filled with the awareness of Christ's peace."

The labyrinth is set within the Retreat Center's 50 wooded acres and it is wheelchair accessible. It is of medieval design with six circuits and it is 90 feet in diameter.

Follow the driveway to the right of all the buildings (south) until reaching the parking lot. Enter through the gate and follow the path. The labyrinth is to the left. There are excellent signs to follow.

Visitors are welcome every day from sunrise to sunset.

**CONTACT:**

Office
860.521.0440 ext.105
hfretreat@holyfamilyretreat.org
www.holyfamilyretreat.org

**NOTES:**

_____

_____

_____

_____

_____

_____

_____

_____

_____

_____

_____

_____

_____

_____

# 43

# Mercy Community Health Inc.

## 2021 Albany Avenue, West Hartford, CT 06117

This labyrinth was dedicated on October 20, 2016, in honor of Sister Maureen Reardon who championed its creation for The Mercy Community. The Palliative Care Center at Saint Mary Home has as its mission the reduction of severity of symptoms of chronic pain in order to empower residents physically, emotionally, socially, and spiritually. Outside space for contemplation was connected to that initiative and the idea of a labyrinth followed.

One of the architects of The Maureen M. Reardon, RSM, Ph.D. Labyrinth at Saint Mary Home is a Sister of Mercy who was involved in designing the labyrinth at Mercy Center in Madison, CT. For this project, she helped determine the style, size, and most importantly, its handicap accessibility.

The Labyrinth is 50 feet in diameter with six circuits and was created using stone pavers, wrought iron lampposts, and materials from the former convent of the Sisters.

To visit, follow the long driveway from Albany Avenue to The Mercy Community parking lot. From the north end of the parking lot, it is a short walk to the labyrinth and garden.

**CONTACT:**

Christine Looby
860.570.8305
clooby@mchct.org
www.themercycommunity.org

**NOTES:**

_____

_____

_____

_____

_____

_____

_____

_____

_____

_____

_____

# 44

# VA Connecticut Healthcare System

## 950 Campbell Avenue, West Haven, CT 06416

This very special labyrinth was created for the Veterans' Hospital, by Martha Haeseler, ATR-BC, director of an outpatient psychiatry program called Giant Steps. In addition to providing art therapy, she helped develop a gardening program in which Veterans create and maintain gardens throughout the VA grounds. Having these gardens available helps patients deal with a wide variety of issues, and has proven to be a powerful form of therapy.

In the spring of 2014, the proposal for a labyrinth was submitted to the VA Director along with a list of endorsements from every VA service department. The approval came in late October, 2014. Martha worked almost non-stop with the help of Giant Step members, other staff, and several devoted Veterans who worked on weekends. The labyrinth was completed in 21 days and dedicated on Veteran's Day.

It is designed with three circuits and modeled after the one in the Chartres Cathedral in France. The 42-foot labyrinth fits comfortably within the central courtyard. The grass paths are 36 inches wide, with six-foot turning areas to accommodate wheelchairs. The central circle is 12 feet wide and contains a mosaic bench made by a Veteran. The paths are demarcated by 18-inch garden beds lined with large granite cobblestones.

The Recreation and Creative Arts Therapy and Chaplain Services supported the project, the Facilities Management Service paid for the granite blocks, and the Patient Experience Committee paid for some of the plants. Martha brought other plants from her garden, some of which she had received years before from her father, who was a U.S. Army Veteran. They used mostly low perennials, grasses, herbs, and bulbs, chosen for three-season interest, color, and scent. Boxwoods provide structure at intersections of the design as well as winter interest. Annuals provide additional color.

Like many hospital labyrinths across the country, this one is proving to benefit patients, visitors, and staff members with their individual challenges.

Access to the public is limited so be sure to check-in, during business hours, at the front desk to obtain a visitor pass or call the Office of Public Affairs number listed below to arrange your visit.

### CONTACT:

Pamela R. Redmond
Public Affairs
203.937.3824
pamela.redmond@va.gov
https://www.connecticut.va.gov

**NOTES:**

# 45

# St. Mark the Evangelist Roman Catholic Church

## 222 McVeagh Road, Westbrook, CT 06498

In 2003, seven women of the St. Mark's Garden Group became interested in building an outdoor labyrinth on the church grounds. Their goal was to provide a cross-cultural, non-denominational opportunity for spiritual growth for the individuals of the Westbrook, CT area by providing a serene environment which would encourage meditation, insight, and celebration. They determined that the labyrinth needed to be permanent, require minimal maintenance, be located close to the parking lot, and have level paths for wheelchair access. They wanted to create an attractive labyrinth that blended into the natural beauty of the surroundings and offer public access during daylight hours.

Funds were raised from sales of tee shirts and Christmas cookies, the publication of a church cookbook, and congregation donations.

Additionally, a $7,500 grant was provided by The Westbrook Foundation.

In 2004, site work began. Professionals were hired to remove two trees, and parishioners cleared brush and graded the area. The concrete paver labyrinth was constructed by GEM Hardscapes during the fall and winter of 2006. Benches, shrubs, flowers, and grass projects where completed in spring, 2007. The Garden Group continues to enhance and maintain the area around the labyrinth.

Since its completion, the labyrinth has received many visitors and garnered a great deal of publicity. Each summer, the church holds a Labyrinth Mass and pot luck dinner. Facilitated walks are offered as well as Lenten walks.

It is easy to find, located just off the north end of the upper parking lot.

**CONTACT:**

Julia Gallicchio
860.388.5186
jdgall@comcast.net
www.stjohnstmark.org

**NOTES:**

_____

_____

_____

_____

# 46

# Saugatuck Congregational Church

## 245 Post Road East, Westport, CT 06880

For many years, members of Saugatuck Congregational Church had been anxious to build a labyrinth on the church property that would be open to anyone interested in taking its spiritual route. A confluence of events eventually made it a reality. A surplus of bricks from a recent church renovation, stored in the church parking lot, gave impetus for the idea to use them. When Liam Borner, a Saugatuck Church member, and confirmand, was considering various Eagle Scout projects, he thought the labyrinth construction would be ideal. Several other church members became involved to offer support, and the result was the Saugatuck Labyrinth project.

A dowser, who had assisted another church member in building a Labyrinth, spent a weekend in Westport, offering a slideshow and lecture presentation. She also taught a workshop on dowsing, while guiding a group of about a dozen people to lay out what would become the Saugatuck Labyrinth.

Over the course of several weekends, members and friends of the Saugatuck Congregational Church, the Boy Scout Troop, and Troop representatives completed the installation of the permanent labyrinth in a special tree-lined section off the front lawn of the church. Close to 200 hours of labor went into the tedious process of digging trenches and laying individual bricks. The result was a classical designed labyrinth 60 feet in diameter with seven circuits.

The path of Saugatuck's Labyrinth is lined with over 1500 individually laid bricks. The optimal location of the rings, the spine and its entrance were determined during the weekend workshop.

All are welcome to visit and walk the labyrinth. It is located under a large tree on a knoll in front of the church on the southeast corner of the property.

**CONTACT:**

Meredith Lederer
203.277.1261

merlederer@msn.com
http://saugatuckchurch.org

**NOTES:**

_____

_____

_____

_____

_____

_____

# 47

# Eastern Connecticut State University

## High Street, Willimantic, CT 06226

*Photo Credit: Carol Williams*

The labyrinth at Eastern Connecticut State University is a seven-circuit seed pattern, 36-foot diameter design. It was constructed in 2006 and represents a lasting legacy of Day for Women, an annual event first held in 1978 which was continued at Eastern for over 25 years by Associate Dean Carol Williams. In 2002, at Day for Women, Ann Ameling held a workshop entitled "Walking a Healing Path" using her 42-foot portable canvas labyrinth (a replica of the Chartres labyrinth in France).

Inspired by the success of that first workshop, the Day for Women team later constructed their own portable labyrinth out of tarps and duct tape. The idea for a permanent labyrinth at Eastern was sparked when Carol Williams walked the beautiful granite labyrinth at New Harmony, Indiana. It occurred to her that a permanent labyrinth would be a wonderful addition to Eastern's campus.

At a subsequent Day for Women event, then President of the University, David G. Carter, became convinced that a permanent labyrinth should be installed at Eastern. After several years of anticipation, a secluded site was chosen near the University's arboretum. Two women in Eastern's Facilities Department, Director Nancy Tinker, and Nancy Harper were responsible for bringing the labyrinth to fruition at its current location. Constructed of brick pavers and grass, it was completed in 2006. The labyrinth is enhanced with reclaimed granite plinths that mark the entrance and were also used to construct Asian inspired benches.

Eastern's labyrinth is open to the public and is wheelchair accessible. It is located across from the Cervantes Parking Garage on Charter Oak Road, which is easily accessed from High Street in Willimantic. Visitors can obtain a temporary parking permit or can visit on weekends when no pass is required. The University invites all persons seeking inspiration and solace to walk Eastern's beautiful labyrinth.

**CONTACT:**

universityrelations@easternct.edu
860.465.5735
https://www.easternct.edu

NOTES:

# 48

# Browns Harvest

## 1911 Poquonock Avenue, Windsor, CT 06095

Browns Harvest is a sixth-generation family farm and a wonderful location for a labyrinth. One of the owners had a feeling that she should bring a labyrinth to the property. In 2016, she created a spiral labyrinth 100 feet in diameter with hay bales next to a classic old tobacco drying shed. Each of the cardinal compass directions is marked with a stake each having a wrapped tobacco leaf "offering." Stones gathered from around the farm also mark sections of the paths. The labyrinth was opened and dedicated during the Full Moon of August 2016.

All who visit will enjoy the farm and its offerings in addition to the spiral labyrinth. It is open seasonally and available during the Farm Stand business hours. However, it is a good idea to call in advance as the property can be muddy at times. This is a large spiral, so be sure to plan your time accordingly.

**CONTACT:**

Kathleen Martin
860.688.1343
brownsharvest@yahoo.com
www.brownsharvest.com

**NOTES:**

_____

_____

_____

_____

_____

_____

_____

_____

_____

_____

_____

_____

_____

# 49

# First Church of Christ

## 5 Meetinghouse Lane, Woodbridge, CT 06525

The First Church labyrinth was inspired by visiting Wisdom House in Litchfield with a communion class. They were very interested in the concept and practices the labyrinth offered. This resulted in research by the group into the history as well as how to construct a labyrinth. At the same time, a couple of large trees in the church's side yard had been lost leaving a clearing just the right size for a labyrinth.

A church leader of the communion class has commented that "one of the virtues of a labyrinth is that though it may be in open space, it allows you a private experience."

Church members were asked to contribute rocks and bricks, from their homes, which represented something meaningful in their lives. These were used to create the border of the pathways. The resulting 45-foot diameter labyrinth with seven circuits is patterned after the one at Wisdom House.

The completed labyrinth was dedicated in 2004 to Pastor Emeritus Boyd M. Johnson, Jr.

The labyrinth will be found to the right of the church just steps from the driveway. It is available to all during daylight hours.

**CONTACT:**

Church Office
203.389.2119
office@uccw.org

**NOTES:**

# 50

# First Congregational Church
# of Woodstock

546 Route 169, Woodstock, CT 06281

The church had, for many years a Children's Center daycare operation, which used their 65x90 backyard as a play area, fenced, with playground equipment and a thick layer of play sand. Following the Center's closure, the area sat derelict and depressing for several years.

Deacon Leslie Sweetnam had always enjoyed the beautifully-situated 11-circuit traditional labyrinth just off Corn Road on the north end of Block Island, with its long view of the sea. He found he liked to walk along the curving circuit before turning, as it was less distracting to his meditation than the Chartres design.

He decided to convert the play area into a labyrinth for the benefit of the whole community. He graded and added sand and trucked 5- to 12- inch rocks from his aptly-named Rocky Hill Road residence. He used his own system to layout a 60-foot labyrinth using many different compass centers and rope lengths.

At the urging of a young church congregant, he altered the design to create a center large enough to accommodate a small wedding party.

He reports that when walking it, several times a week, he often finds unfamiliar footprints in the sand, sometimes small footprints playfully cheating back and forth between paths. The path alternates between sand and grass, referencing the changes in our life's paths. Some weeks the grass is more freshly trimmed than others.

The church is easy to find, a lovely traditional steepled meetinghouse across from The Pink House, Roseland Cottage, at the south end of the common, adjacent to the large cemetery. The labyrinth is located in the rear churchyard within a white fence. Like the open and affirming UCC church it is a part, the path is always open and welcoming to all.

**CONTACT:**

G. Leslie Sweetnam
860.974.2032
glsweetnam@att.net
http://firstchurchwoodstock.org/labyrinth/

NOTES:

_____

_____

_____

_____

# RHODE ISLAND

# 1

# The Turning Point

746 Corn Neck Road, New Shoreham/Block Island, RI
02807

This is arguably one of the most well-known labyrinths in New
England and certainly in Rhode Island. Barbara MacDougall had a
series of encounters with labyrinths beginning with her neighbor's,
built in 1997. This led to the creation of the labyrinth at The
Turning Point. It was designed by Mary Cain and built in the
spring of 2001 with the help of those attending a spiritual workshop
there. Many of the rocks used were recycled from the neighbor's
labyrinth, which had been abandoned following the sale of the
property. The medieval design with 11 circuits encompasses a good
deal of real estate. The location on a knoll overlooking New Harbor
and Block Island Sound is spectacular.

In 2003, a sculpture garden was added. Located beneath a nearby
apple tree is a box containing a journal for visitors to write their
reflections. In 2009, several past entries were reproduced in a
delightful book entitled, Letters from the Labyrinth. The

introduction by Barbara MacDougal provides a more detailed history of the site.

The labyrinth can be found on the free tourist map of Block Island. Its location 3.5 miles from town can make it a bit cumbersome to reach. This, however, is not a deterrent with 50-75 people arriving daily in season on foot, by bike, or taxi. Follow Corn Neck Road north out of town - the Labyrinth sign is on the left. There is a wooden stairway crossing the stone wall. It is available during daylight hours.

No Contact Information at this time.

**NOTES:**

_____

_____

_____

_____

_____

_____

_____

_____

_____

_____

# 2

# Emmanuel Episcopal Church

120 Nate Whipple Way, Cumberland, RI 02864

Emmanuel Church has been blessed with a large campus. In the fall of 2014, a group of parishioners cleared out a portion of the property, leaving a rocky piece of ground where once-crowded trees now flourish.

They decided that the land should be used in a way that could bring joy and solace to anyone who wanted to come and walk, read, reflect, meditate, or pray. In the spring of 2015, the parish held a capital campaign to raise funds to have a Prayer and Meditation Garden designed and built by Magma Designs. Within the larger garden are six distinct spaces: a Welcome Garden, an Intention Garden, a Reflection Garden, a Memorial Garden, a Meadow Garden, and a Labyrinth. Each mini-garden is dedicated to individuals or groups, with benches provided throughout. In 2017, a Little Free Library was added.

The labyrinth has a diameter of 32 feet, and is a variation on the classic six-circuit design called a Chalice Labyrinth. The path is mulch, and the outline is stone. Although the ground was prepared, and the design traced out by experts, it was members and many children who got together to carefully lay out the stones. The labyrinth is dedicated to those who have lost children.

To access the labyrinth, follow the drive to the far end of the parking area. The labyrinth is part of the meditation garden, tucked into the wooded area on your left. All are welcome during daylight hours.

**CONTACT:**

The Rev. Joan Testin
401.658.1506
vicarjoan@gmail.com
http://emmanuelri.org

**NOTES:**

_____

_____

_____

_____

_____

_____

_____

_____

# 3

# Shepard of the Valley
# United Methodist Church

604 Seven Mile Road, Hope, RI 02877

This 60-foot diameter labyrinth was created through a series of fortuitous occurrences. With a vague dream of a labyrinth behind the church, the pastor's husband cleared the overgrown field one spring. Soon after came a call from the leader of a youth group from the First United Methodist Church in Wilkesboro, N.C. Their youth group was looking for a mission to perform on a trip. When told of the labyrinth idea, they became extremely interested, but the church had no budget to cover the material costs.

Nevertheless, the pastor and a friend, using rope, laid out a pattern for the youths to follow when they arrived. A passerby who was told of the potential labyrinth volunteered to pay for all the costs. She had once used a labyrinth during a period of recovery from cancer treatment and had found it healing. The result is a lovely pattern with wide meandering pathways.

Another fortuitous occurrence was when an Eagle Scout in search of a project offered to build a fire pit with benches. He thoughtfully made the benches high enough for seniors to use comfortably. This now provides a wonderful complement to the labyrinth and a place to pause and reflect.

For scheduled events, contact the church or visit their website.

Park in the lot behind the church. Follow the path which leads from the northeast corner of the lot to the huge grass labyrinth and neighboring fire pit area. The Labyrinth is open sun up to sundown seven days a week.

**CONTACT:**

Rev. Katherine Mitchell
401.821.8217
office@sovumc.necoxmail.com
https://www.sovumc.org

**NOTES:**

_____

_____

_____

_____

_____

_____

_____

# 4

# St Augustine's
# Episcopal Center at URI

15 Lower College Road, Kingston, RI 02881

This labyrinth was given to St. Augustine's by an anonymous donor in early 2017, and constructed in the spring and summer of that year. It was designed by Grandin Landscape & Supply Company of Wakefield, RI. The planting scheme was designed by Jane Vachon, a landscape designer, and Hiroko Shimizu, a parishioner of St. Augustine's. The traditional design is executed with large irregular thick stone pavers to form the pathways with flower borders consisting of Astilbe, Heuchera, Ajuga, Alchemilla, Wild Ginger, Lamium, and Primrose. This creates a shifting color scheme of rose, deep russet purple, pale yellow, light blue, and gray-green against a green moss ground. The labyrinth is surrounded by a low box border. It has medieval and rustic characteristics appropriate for its setting in St Augustine's natural, slightly undisciplined church garden which is beside a perennial stream. The labyrinth, located in a secluded spot on the east side of the church, is bordered by large smooth stone outcrops. The parish memorial garden is across the stream and is accessed by a small wooden bridge.

There is parking in front of the church unless there is a service. The labyrinth and garden are located behind the church and are available during daylight hours.

**CONTACT:**

Cheryl Petrosinelli
401.783.2153
staugustinesadmin@necoxmail.com
https://staugustineuri.org

**NOTES:**

_____

_____

_____

_____

_____

_____

_____

_____

_____

_____

_____

# Calvary United Methodist Church

## 200 Turner Road, Middletown, RI 02842

This unpretentious three-circuit labyrinth is 19 feet in diameter and is based on the Cretan design. Located at the entrance, it offers a warm welcome to all who visit the church. It was designed and built by a young parishioner, Jonah Emerson, for his Eagle Scout Project in 2015. A stone bench has been placed in the center, which offers a serene place to reflect.

The labyrinth is easily accessible from the church parking lot and it is available during daylight hours. All are welcome.

**CONTACT:**

Church Secretary
401.847.6181
calvaryadmin@necoxmail.com
http://www.middletownmethodist.com

# St. Peter's by-the-Sea

## 72 Central Street, Narragansett, RI 02882

This picturesque labyrinth is situated in the historic district of Narragansett at St. Peter's by the Sea Episcopal Church. The church was founded in 1869, but the original wood-frame building was destroyed the same year by a great northeast gale. The present stone building was erected, consecrated, and opened for worship in 1873. Additional buildings were later added including the bell tower.

Nestled in a corner at the intersection of the bell tower and guildhall, a memorial garden was created many years ago. A brass plaque mounted on the church wall memorializes past parishioners. The garden was bordered by a boxwood hedge which failed to withstand the strong ocean air. The small garden committee was unable to keep the flower beds healthy.

In 2013, a woman who had recently joined the church saw the neglected Memorial Garden and envisioned a prayer path of sorts.

Though inexperienced with labyrinths, she felt compelled to research the idea, subsequently feeling that the space required one. She engaged another parishioner/gardener and together they researched ideas, visited other labyrinths, and decided on a plan. The restrictions of the space demanded a small labyrinth, and in keeping with the gothic architecture, a medieval three-circuit design was chosen.

A landscaper was engaged to do the heavy work, and he used the cobblestones already there to outline the paths. Small stones were used to fill the pathway. The plantings surrounding the area were chosen to be sustainable in the ocean side location. The labyrinth is bordered on three sides by a small hedge of ilex crenata. The inside corners have plantings of fragrant Nepeta (catmint). The fourth side, at the entrance, has a beautiful row of Veronica (speedwell). The entire space, by virtue of its repetition of elements and restful blue color scheme, provides just the meditative atmosphere conducive to prayer and reflection.

Adjacent to the small cobblestone apron which serves as the entranceway is a stone carved with a dedication to Edith Noyes Knight "Nod" Meyer, a renowned local horticulturalist, whose family's memorial gift made the labyrinth possible. Completing the tranquil garden is a stone bench facing the labyrinth under the shade of an ancient dogwood tree.

The labyrinth is open to the public during daylight hours.

**CONTACT:**

office@stpetersbythesea.com
401.783.4623
http://stpetersbythesea.com

# Salve Regina University

## 100 Ochre Point Avenue, Newport, RI 02840

Sister Leona Misto, former Vice President for Mission Integration, designed and built the labyrinth at Salve Regina University in response to students expressed desire to have a serene place to contemplate life and relieve stress.

The seven-circuit Chartres-styled labyrinth (credit: Labyrinth Company St. Paul à la Chartres™) is beautifully situated with three large Copper Beach trees surrounding it. It is a short walk from the corner of Ochre Point Avenue and Leroy Avenue directly east of Gerety Hall on the grounds of the Wakehurst estate.

**CONTACT:**

Kristine Hendrickson
401.341.2148
https://salve.edu/
hendrick@salve.edu

# Sod Maze

Chateau-sur-Mer

424 Bellevue Avenue, Newport, RI 02840

*Photo Credit: The Preservation Society of Newport County*

When considering the city of Newport, RI, most visitors will think of the impressive architecture of its many mansions as well as their surrounding landscapes. The beautiful property of Chateau-sur-Mer is an excellent example of how well-designed and engineered grounds can appear to be wild and natural. It is also home to Richard Fleischner's Sod Maze, the only remaining installation created for the city-wide Monumenta art exhibition of 1974. This labyrinth has the distinction of being the oldest one listed in this guide.

Visiting hours and fees can be found on the Preservation Society's website.

**CONTACT:**

The Preservation Society of Newport County
401.847.1000
www.newportmansions.org

**NOTES:**

_____

_____

_____

_____

_____

_____

_____

_____

_____

_____

_____

_____

_____

_____

_____

_____

_____

# 9

# Central Congregational Church - United Church of Christ

## 296 Angell Street, Providence, RI 02906

This beautiful labyrinth (credit: Labyrinth Company, Chelsea™) was dedicated to The Reverend Rebecca Spencer, Senior Minister, for her 25 years of faithful service to the Central Congregational Church, UCC.

The area around this labyrinth is very nicely landscaped and includes a sitting wall for meditation, which was completed in 2013. This is a compact labyrinth comprised of six circuits within its 17-foot diameter. As it is small, at each bend, users will often do a breath prayer or other meditative breathing technique, read a bit of Scripture, or practice mind-emptying.

Located behind the church in the area bordered by the kitchen and the Church School wing, it is best accessed by the walkway, next to the Nursery School, which leads from Stimson Avenue, a one-way between Hope Street and Diman Place. There is free street parking. The labyrinth is available to all during daylight hours.

In addition to the outdoor labyrinth, a larger, Chartres-styled indoor version, created in 2002, is painted on the floor of the Makepeace Room. This is a multipurpose space, so please contact the church in advance to arrange your visit to the labyrinth.

**CONTACT:**

Church Secretary
401.331.1960
cccangell@centralchurch.us
https://www.centralchurch.us

**NOTES:**

_____

_____

_____

_____

_____

_____

_____

_____

_____

_____

# 10

# The Church of the Redeemer

655 Hope Street, Providence, RI 02906

Founded in 1859, The Church of the Redeemer is located in a residential section of Providence. The labyrinth on the front lawn facing Hope Street, a quiet refuge, surrounded by trees that welcomes all passersby.

The design is a free-form pattern 25 feet in diameter and was created by a formerly assigned priest, Reverend Jo-Ann Drake, who was inspired by the experience of walking portable labyrinths during workshops. She wanted to offer a permanent labyrinth to both parishioners and area residents. In 2000, she and members of the parish laid out the pattern in lime before installing the red paving stones in the earth. The centerpiece, a stained-glass cross set in concrete, was created by the Church's property manager.

The Bishop, the Reverend Geralyn Wolf, dedicated the labyrinth to be used as a place where people can come to pray, to think about God, or just come to find peace.

The labyrinth is always available, and all are welcome.

**CONTACT:**

The Reverend Patrick A. Campbell
401.331.0678
pcampbell@redeemerprovidence.org
www.redeemerprovidence.org

**NOTES:** _____

_____

_____

_____

_____

_____

_____

_____

_____

_____

_____

_____

_____

_____

_____

_____

# 11

# Grace Episcopal Church

300 Westminster Street, Providence, RI 02903

Built in 1846, Grace Episcopal Church is located in downtown Providence at 300 Westminster Street. In 2017, The Pavilion at Grace was added as the church's new parish hall and event space. Designed by Centerbrook Architects and constructed by Bowerman Associates, it is located next to the church and at ground level to allow easy access to the disabled.

The patio area which includes the labyrinth and garden fronts Westminster Street. Because of the shape of this space, the labyrinth was created using an unusual, visually interesting square design. The border stones are six inches wide, with the path delineated by 18-inch wide stones.

Though the space is fenced on the street side, the front doors of Grace Church are open each weekday from 11:00 am – 2:00 pm as part of their Open Doors Ministry. To access the labyrinth at other times, inquire at the reception office located around back facing the church's parking lot on Chapel Street. The office is open Monday-Friday from 9:00am-5:00 pm.

**CONTACT:**

Chris Barker
401.331.3225
thepavillion@gracepvd.org
http://www.gracechurchprovidence.org

NOTES:

_____

_____

_____

_____

_____

_____

_____

_____

_____

_____

_____

_____

_____

# 12

# Sunrose Farm

495 Gilbert Stuart Road, Saunderstown, RI 02874

Sybil Rose and Stephen Pierce have been manifesting a dream of making their farm a place where people can come, lighten their hearts, find a moment of peace and, experience their inner knowing. Their labyrinth, located in a field behind the house, was created in 2014. The seven circuits of the 60-foot diameter labyrinth were created by Stephen's careful mowing of the grass.

The owner's intention of creating a labyrinth containing seven circuits that follows The Lord's Prayer, came in part from the book The Source of All Miracles, by Kathleen McGowan, as well as from impressions received during meditation. The seven chakras of the body and elemental symbols were also factors.

Placed alongside the paths of each circuit are signposts with poems written by Sybil Pierce for reflection on each of the seven steps in the book - faith, surrender, service, abundance, forgiveness, overcoming, and love.

Sybil and Stephen have also created a spiral labyrinth made with herbs and flowers.

Please call to schedule your visit and to learn more about Sunrose Farm.

**CONTACT:**

Sybil Pierce
401.295.4070
sybilrose495@gmail.com
https://sunrosefarmri.com

NOTES:

_____

_____

_____

_____

_____

_____

_____

_____

_____

_____

_____

# 13

# Fagan Park

### 100 Dam Street, South Kingston, RI 02879

*Photo Credit: Alyssa Hiener*

Fagan Park is located adjacent to the South County Bike Path in Peace Dale Village. The park was renovated to compliment both the bike path and the local neighborhood. Changes included adding picnic tables, a water fountain, swings, and, landscaping improvements. In 2017 the 24-foot diameter, five-circuit labyrinth was added by a local girl scout who wanted to bring a useful symbol of peace to the community. It is a lovely addition located in a quiet, shaded area of the park where a tranquil walk awaits.

Alyssa Hiener, the creator of the labyrinth, wrote: "I created the Peace Labyrinth at Fagan Park for my Girl Scout Silver Award in the summer of 2017. I had just entered my freshman year in High School and recently bridged from Cadette to Senior in Girl Scouts. My Labyrinth was created to address the amount of negativity in my community. I chose to make this labyrinth because of the tremendous amount of bullying and violence around the world. I wanted to create a place to unwind and just walk, to clear their mind."

She has succeeded in creating a welcoming environment in which visitors may calm their souls and clear their minds. This little peaceful corner of the park will surely help spread goodwill.

Easy access to the labyrinth is from Dam Street where you will be able to see it from the parking area. It is available during park hours.

**CONTACT:**

Parks and Recreation Department
401.789.9301
http://parksandrec.southkingstownri.com/

NOTES:

_____

_____

_____

_____

_____

_____

_____

_____

_____

_____

# 14

# Pilgrim Lutheran Church

## 1817 Warwick Avenue, Warwick, RI 02889

In 2006, Divinity School Intern Tiffany Hopkins, wishing to share the peace and clarity she had discovered from walking labyrinths, proposed building one for the church. The congregation was enthusiastic about the idea and soon set about making the necessary arrangements. In the heat of the summer, weeks of hard work followed to prepare the site. One Saturday, dozens of volunteers working together laid the granite stones and filled in tons of stone dust as the final phase of creating the six-circuit domed patterned labyrinth. An Abingdon™ pattern from The Labyrinth Company was used.

On Holy Saturday, a fire pit is placed at the center of the labyrinth. An evening Easter Vigil begins with a labyrinth walk and is followed with a procession indoors for the remainder of the observance.

It is available during daylight hours

**CONTACT:**

Parish Assistant
401.739.2937
parishasst@pilgrimlutheranri.org
pilgrimlutheranri.jimdo.com

**NOTES:**

# Labyrinth Resources

Below are just a few of the resources available. Many more will be found online.

**The Labyrinth Society**
P.O. Box 736
Trumansburg, NY 14886
607.387.5863 (accepts voice mail only)
info@labyrinthsociety.org
https://labyrinthsociety.org

**Labyrinths of New England**
Belfast, ME
207.922.7542
yadina.clark@gmail.com
https://yadinaclark.wixsite.com/labyrinthsne

**Veriditas**
101 H Street, Suite D
Petaluma, CA 94952
707.283.0373
contact@veriditas.org
https://www.veriditas.org/

**The Labyrinth Company**
244 Watch Hill Road
Kensington, CT 06037-3657 USA
888.715.2297
info@labyrinthcompany.com
http://www.labyrinthcompany.com/

**Paths of Peace**
P.O. Box 701
Stillwater, MN 55082-0701
612.747.7446

pathsofpeace@gmail.com
http://www.pathsofpeace.com/

*Books:*

Walking a Sacred Path: Rediscovering the Labyrinth as a Spiritual Practice
by Lauren Artress

Labyrinths & Mazes: A Journey Through Art, Architecture, and Landscape (includes 250 photographs of ancient and modern labyrinths and mazes from around the world)
by Francesca Tatarella

Church Labyrinths: Questions and answers regarding the history, relevance, and use of labyrinths in churches
by Robert D. Ferre

The Labyrinth Revival
by Robert Ferre

"Kids on the Path"
School Labyrinth Guide
by Marge McCarthy

Walking the Labyrinth: Your Path to Peace and Possibilities
by Diana Ng

Labyrinth: Landscape of the Soul
by Di Williams

## About the Author

Bill Ludwig, a Connecticut native, began life in Woodbridge, CT and is now a long-time resident of Branford, CT. He was a partner for 28 years with Garland Publishing, an academic and science publisher, where he filled various roles as the company grew from its founding in 1969 until its sale in 1997. Following the sale, he took a few years to pursue his love of sailing and travel, obtaining a captain's license. He sailed the east coast Maine to Florida on his own sailboat, Blue Moon, and captained many boats for others. He has made three trips to Bermuda.

Once settled back on land, he tried his hand at a variety of business before returning to what he knew best, publishing. He founded Hotchkiss Publishing in 2014. This led to a sequence of events guiding him to become interested in labyrinths and he began looking for them wherever he traveled. In the fall of 2017, prior to walking the Camino de Santiago, from Lourdes France, he decided that upon his return he would create a guide book to the labyrinths of CT & RI. Little did he realize that his love of labyrinths would lead him to find the love of his life when he walked one of the few labyrinths along the Camino with a Dutch woman and fell in love. Creating this book took a bit longer than expected as it was interrupted by frequent trips to the Netherlands.

Chasing Labyrinths, Bill's first book was much more work that he had envisioned as well as more rewarding. However, he looks forward to chasing more labyrinths in New England and elsewhere.

# Also by Hotchkiss Publishing

**Dear Friend 1 & Dear Friend 2** – Meditations and Journal for Your Spiritual Journey by Sandy Beach

A respected AA speaker, Sandy was well known as a spiritual "seeker". Volume 1 was published for his 50<sup>th</sup>

anniversary, December 7, 2014, Pearl Harbor Day. Volume 2 continues with the last of his written meditations. Each volume offers weekly meditations and journal.

**Steps and Stories** – History, Steps, and Spirituality of Alcoholics Anonymous by Sandy Beach

Sandy considered this to be his quintessential work. He recounts the confluences of people that lead up to Bill W. and Dr. Bob's first meeting and tells little known stories from early AA history. Sandy offers a message of home in a way which makes spirituality a desirable goal and accessible to all.

# Also by Hotchkiss Publishing

**Bottoms Up** – A Recovery by Paul C.

Paul C. was an accomplished journalist and photographer, an Adams, Mass. native. Paul tells his "story" through a series of engaging vignettes. This, his third book, is his legacy. He passed way, 37 years in recovery, May 2016, having just completed "Bottoms Up".

**Hangover** – Illustrated by Alex Kenné with Commentary by Robert Gibson

Artist Alex Kenné illustrates the painful journey through the various stages of the dreaded hangover. Very brief commentary, often a single word is provided by Robert Gibson. Originally published in 1948, now available in facsimile for you to have fun with. Makes a great gift.

All titles available from Amazon. Or contact the publisher for more information at info@hotchkisspublishing.com.

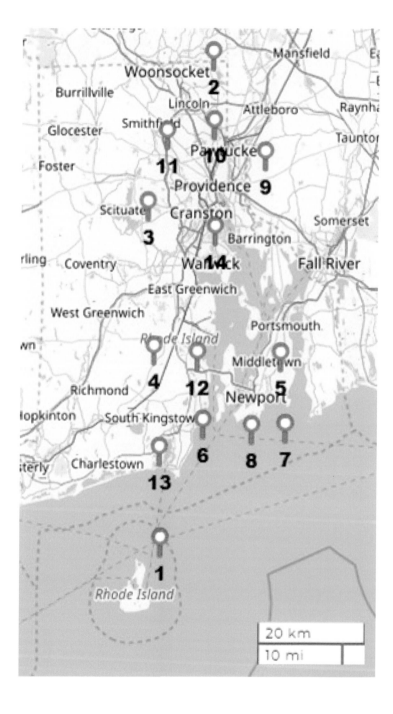